DK Metcalf: The Inspiring Story of One of Football's Star Wide Receivers

An Unauthorized Biography

By: Clayton Geoffreys

Table of Contents

Foreword

It's not easy to receive for over 1,000 yards in the NFL, but DK Metcalf has done that on several occasions over his professional football career. Since being selected in the 2019 NFL Draft by the Seattle Seahawks, Metcalf has quickly become a top wide receiver in the league, being selected to the Pro Bowl in 2020. There is still a lot more to come in Metcalf's career in the years ahead. Thank you for purchasing *DK Metcalf: The Inspiring Story of One of Football's Star Wide Receivers*. In this unauthorized biography, we will learn DK Metcalf's incredible life story and impact on the game of football. Hope you enjoy and if you do, please do not forget to leave a review!

Also, check out my website at claytongeoffreys.com to join my exclusive list where I let you know about my latest books. To thank you for your purchase, you can go to my site to download a free copy of *33 Life Lessons: Success Principles, Career Advice & Habits of Successful People.* In the book, you'll learn from some of the greatest thought leaders of different industries on what it takes to become successful and how to live a great life.

Cheers,

Clayton Geoffreys

Visit me at www.claytongeoffreys.com

Introduction

If you've never been around an NFL player, one of the things that is hard to fathom is their immense size. The average man in the United States stands at 5'9" and weighs 198 pounds. Pretty standard for the everyday man. When you watch games on Sundays, the smallest players on the field are the punters and kickers. For the most part, punters and kickers only average 10-15 plays a game. But in comparison to their teammates, they look tiny.

That said, even the average NFL kicker and punter is larger than the typical American man. The average NFL kicker stands at six feet, a full three inches taller than the average American, and weighs 203 pounds. The average NFL punter stands at 6'1" and weighs 214 pounds. But when you see them standing on the sideline next to the other players, they look like children amongst grown men. Even the smallest players on an NFL roster are larger than the average

American man. And those are just the smallest players; imagine the size of the largest players!

Offensive linemen are the largest men on an NFL roster, averaging nearly 6'5" and 314 pounds. That's a human being the size of a doorway—a full nine inches and 116 pounds heavier than the average American.

So, what makes these humans so monstrous? It is usually hours upon hours spent in the weight room. For NFL players, their bodies are their livelihoods, so they must maintain their physiques or risk losing their jobs. But there is more to playing in the league than just being exceptionally large. There are any number of former NFL football players who were monster-sized human beings but could not master the mental side of the game.

So, if an NFL player needs both the physical and the mental parts of the game, how does one determine if someone is going to be a successful player once they get into the league? In the end, it becomes a crap shoot, and teams have to go on the best information available to them at the time.

There are dozens of future Hall-of-Famers who dropped low in the draft for various reasons, only to have tremendous NFL careers. Perhaps they were a step too slow or did not do well in their interviews. But once they got into the league, they were able to dominate the NFL.

Wide receiver DK Metcalf was one of those who fell in the draft because of injury concerns, and he was slow running his cone drill. Tom Brady, who had a legendarily bad combine, was actually faster than Metcalf in the cone drill.

But what Metcalf did have was the size and the NFL pedigree. The average wide receiver in the NFL is six foot and a little over 200 pounds. Metcalf stands at 6'4" and weighs just over 240 pounds of pure muscle. He claims that he has less than two percent body fat.

Besides his massive size advantage over opposing defensive backs, Metcalf was also given another advantage at birth. His father was a former-college All-American and NFL player. This allowed DK to be around college and professional players since the day he was born.

DK Metcalf was born in Oxford, Mississippi, on December 14, 1997. At the time, both his father Terrence and his mother Tanya were in high school. Terrence Metcalf received a football scholarship to play at the University of Mississippi, which was in the same town DK was born.

Terrence often brought DK with him to the Rebels weight room, and the bored kid started lifting weights. Players on the Ole Miss team started calling DK "Lil Muscle" because his biceps were already shaped up when he was born. Terrence claims that before DK was five, he could bench press 50 pounds and squat 100.

After four years at Ole Miss, Terrence was drafted by the Chicago Bears. Young DK, Tanya, and Terrence headed north to the Windy City. While DK was working out in the weight room one day with his dad, the Chicago Bears trainer saw him and told Terrence that using weights was a bad idea for his age. The trainer believed that using free weights would stunt DK's growth, which seems comical now. Instead, he advised DK to work out with resistance bands. It would help to build his strength but also help with his flexibility.

When the Bears won the NFC Championship in 2007, it was DK who carried the George Halas Trophy into the Chicago locker room after the game.

DK was 10 years old when the family moved back to Oxford, Mississippi. Terrence's time with the Bears was over and now was the time for DK to start his own playing career. But Terrence was nervous about letting his son play football. He waited until DK turned 12 before he would allow him to play. Terrence worried that the wrong coach might ruin the game for DK at a young age.

By the time DK entered high school, he excelled at football, basketball, and track. He lifted weights but had not yet become the sculpted figure that we know today. It just so happened that Oxford High School had a state championship-winning powerlifting team led by Jason Russell. It was Russell who got DK serious about lifting weights. Russell created a lifting program for him that would require a year-round commitment. The new program was four days a week, every week of the year, and it wasn't long before it started to show results for DK. During his freshman year, he started on the varsity football team at wide receiver and safety.

During his sophomore season, Oxford made it all the way to the Mississippi 5A State Championship for the first time in school history but lost after giving up 21 unanswered points in the fourth quarter.

It was during that season that Terrence noticed a change in his son. DK was playing against Terrence's former high school, Clarksdale. On the snap, DK started blocking the cornerback in front of him. By the time the whistle blew, DK had blocked him off the field and nearly into the stands. It was at that point that Terrence knew he had created a monster.

By his junior season, DK was starting to get looks from big-time colleges. He received offers from UCLA and Auburn but his heart was in Oxford, like his dad before him.

DK also never had an off-season. He went right from football season to basketball to track. In basketball, he was a star. During his senior season, he averaged a double-double. In track, he set the school record in the triple and high jump and was a part of the 4X100 team that set a Mississippi state record.

During his junior season, he led Oxford High School back to the state championship game, but they lost again.

In the summer between his junior and senior year, DK made his first foray into internet fame by deadlifting 595 pounds. The video made the rounds online, making DK a little famous.

Just before his senior year, DK decided to follow his dad and signed with Ole Miss. He would not have to go that far. The campus was only a few miles away from his house.

For the third straight year, DK led Oxford back to the state championship game, only to lose a heartbreaker again. In three seasons, Oxford lost three straight state championship games by a combined total of just 14 points.

In his freshman season at Ole Miss, DK only caught two passes. On his second reception of the season, he scored a touchdown but came down awkwardly and broke his foot. He would miss the remainder of his freshman year as a result. Nevertheless, both of his catches were for touchdowns.

DK had a stellar redshirt freshman season, but because Ole Miss was on probation, the team could not go to a bowl game. They won their final game of the season against rival Mississippi State in the Egg Bowl.

During his redshirt sophomore season, DK was joined in the Ole Miss wide receiver corps by two other future-NFL stars, A.J. Brown and Elijah Moore. DK was having a great season, but against Arkansas, he suffered a neck injury. He was blocking on a kickoff return and a player on the opposing team's helmet hit him just under the chin. At first, he thought it was just a stinger, a common football injury, but it turned out to be much more.

A CT scan revealed that DK had broken a vertebra and the chipped bone was sitting inside his neck. A few centimeters more and the bone chip would have cut his spine and he would have been paralyzed.

The first doctor DK saw told him that he would never play football again. It was a stunning revelation. He believed that he could have been a great NFL player, but now that seemed to be going away in the blink of an eye. But a second opinion revealed that surgery could fix the problem and he would be back to playing within a few months. And just like that, he was back.

But now, DK had a decision to make. He still had two years of eligibility left, or he could head to the NFL draft. He decided to start training and enter the draft.

With very little tape, DK had to impress scouts at the NFL draft. In some ways, he did, and in others, he failed. DK ran the 40-yard dash in 4.33 seconds and bench-pressed 225 pounds 27 times. But his time in the cone drill was too slow.

As the draft progressed, DK started to slide. He was invited to attend the first round in Nashville, but his name was not called. That night, the Metcalf family returned to Oxford without saying a word. Then, finally, with the last pick in the second round, the Seattle Seahawks called his name.

In his first regular-season game with the Seahawks, DK set the record for most receiving yards by a player in his first career game with the team, breaking Hall-of-Famer Steve Largent's record. It took until Week 9 before DK recorded his first career 100-yard game against the Buccaneers.

In the Wild Card round of the playoffs, DK torched the Philadelphia Eagles, one of the teams that had passed on him in the draft. He recorded 160 receiving yards and a touchdown, setting an NFL record for most receiving yards by a rookie in a playoff game. The Seahawks would lose the following week, ending their season.

During the Covid lockdowns, DK headed to Mexico to spend time with his quarterback, Russell Wilson. The two spent every day together, working on timing and becoming friends.

This quality time in Mexico would show results during the 2020 season, as DK had his best year as a pro. He had 83 receptions for 1,303 yards and 10 touchdowns. He would be named to the Pro Bowl for the first time and was second team All-Pro.

Seattle won the NFC West for the first and only time in DK's career. In the Wild Card round of the playoffs, the Seahawks hosted the Rams and lost by 10 points.

During the offseason, DK qualified for the U.S. Track and Field Olympic trials in the 100-meter. He ended up finishing ninth, missing out on the Olympics by less than .3 seconds.

During the 2021 season, Russell Wilson suffered an injury, and the Seahawks struggled. For the first time in Wilson's career, Seattle had a losing record. Without Wilson, DK's numbers suffered. Then, in the offseason, the Seahawks traded Wilson to the Denver

Broncos. Geno Smith was going to be the new starting quarterback for Seattle. After trading Wilson, Seattle signed DK to a three-year extension worth $72 million.

With a new quarterback, DK's numbers again fell. He did catch a career-high 90 passes, but only 6 touchdowns. But with Smith as the quarterback, Seattle thrived. The offense changed from Wilson's pass-happy throwing attack to Smith's running attack.

The Seahawks made the playoffs for the third time in DK's career but lost in the Wild Card round to the 49ers. DK did catch a touchdown pass in the game. It was his third career touchdown catch of more than 50 yards in the playoffs. That tied him for second all-time with Randy Moss.

DK Metcalf is still only 25 years old at the time of this writing. He will undoubtedly be with the Seattle Seahawks for the next three seasons. After battling back from injury in college, he has not missed a single game in the pros.

After only four seasons in the league, DK Metcalf has established himself as one of the best receivers in the league. His workouts and Instagram workout photos have become legendary online. He was only able to play 21 games in college and is still learning the position. He has shown that he is dedicated to his craft and only continues to get better as an NFL football player. In the years to come, he will show why he is one of the best receivers. Now, he has the challenge of becoming an all-time great.

Chapter 1: Childhood & High School

For some people, football is just in their blood. They are born into the game and it is all they know. Eli and Peyton Manning were destined to be quarterbacks in the NFL. Nick and Joey Bosa had no choice but to be defensive linemen. In both cases, the brothers were preceded in the NFL by their fathers. In the case of the Bosas, their maternal grandfather was also in the NFL.

Having a father that played in the league gives those players a leg up on their competition. They know how much work goes into making it. But it also gives those players a better understanding of the game. They talk about football at the dinner table like other families discuss the weather.

DK's father, Terrence Metcalf, was born in Clarksdale, Mississippi. He became a Parade All-American as an offensive lineman for Clarksdale High School and received a scholarship to play football at the University of Mississippi. During his sophomore year, he was second team All-American, and during his senior year, he was first team All-American.

In the 2002 NFL Draft, the Chicago Bears selected Metcalf in the third round. He played seven seasons with the Bears, starting 25 games. He ended his career in 2010 with the New Orleans Saints.

During Terrence's senior year of high school, his girlfriend and eventual wife, Tonya, got pregnant with the couple's first child. On December 14, 1997, DeKaylin Metcalf was born in Oxford, Mississippi. From the day he was born, DK made quite an impression.

When his father was at Ole Miss, his teammates bestowed a nickname up little DK, "Lil Muscle." It seemed appropriate for a man who would one day say that he had less than two percent body fat.

"He was just a little baby with biceps all shaped up," Terrence said. "He just showed crazy strength when he was a young kid."[i]

Terrence swears that DK could bench 50 pounds and squat 100 pounds before he was five years old, but there is no way to verify that story.

With both of his parents still in high school when he was born, Tonya had to go to work in order to make ends meet while Terrence concentrated on his football career. By the time they left for Ole Miss, Tonya was pregnant with the couple's second child and working full-time at a child daycare center while Terrence played for the Rebels.

When his father was selected by the Chicago Bears, the entire family moved to the Windy City. Tonya quit her job and was now a full-time mother. However, before they left Oxford, Tonya graduated from Ole Miss with a degree in consumer and family sciences.

By this time, Tonya had given birth to a daughter, Zharia. Despite the rigors of being a professional football player, Terrence still worked hard at being a father. He tried to get home every night to have dinner with his family. But it was still in the weight room that father and son bonded.

"Probably every day, when my dad got home from practice," DK said of how often he would hit the weights. "Me just being young and wanting something to do, and just happy to see my dad after practice. That was just something that we did together. I believe that's what made me want to do it so much."[ii]

One day, the Bears' conditioning coach saw Terrence and DK working out in the Chicago weight room. He advised Terrence to stop having young DK work out with free weights, as it might stunt his growth. An amusing statement, given how large DK would one day be!

Instead, the trainer gave Terrence resistance bands for DK. This would allow him to use his muscles while at the same time ensuring his flexibility.

"And then he's like, OK, just go buy bands and let's train him a different way. So, I started him with band workouts at home," Terrence said.[ii]

When DK was nine, the Bears beat the New Orleans Saints in the NFC Championship game and were headed to the Super Bowl. DK carried the George Halas Trophy from the field back to his dad's locker inside Soldier Field. Given his age and the weight of the trophy, young DK had no problem carrying it around.

"I got invited into the locker room, and I got to hold the trophy and celebrate with the players," DK said. "It was really fun to be around."[iii]

But being around players became second nature for DK. He had practically grown up in the Ole Miss locker room, and from there, he went directly into the Chicago Bears locker room. Every step of the way, he was learning the game from some of the best players in the world. DK got to sit in meeting rooms and watch practices, and on occasion, some of the players would even become his coach.

"DK got to be around a lot of guys who were really good at the game," Terrence said. "When he was in about second or third grade, former Bears safety Bobby Gray started working with him. At that age, when you're a parent trying to train your child, they don't want to listen to you, so you get them with someone else. The things he remembers helped him become a better receiver. He remembers all of the passing routes he was taught by the guys in the NFL."[iii]

When he was in Chicago, Tanya thought it was important that DK learn how to swim. She signed him up for a lesson with a group of other children at a local pool. When the time came, all the kids jumped into the water, and one by one, they all popped back up—all of them except DK. He sunk to the bottom of the pool like a rock, and there he stayed until the instructor dove down to the bottom and fished him out. That would be the end of the swimming lesson for that day.

The following week, Tanya and DK went back for another lesson, but he would not get out of the car. He stayed there until Tanya finally agreed to drive him back home. That was the end of swimming lessons.

This one incident caused a profound fear of the water for DK. He was well into his 20s before he finally got over it, with the help of Russell Wilson. While the two were training together in Mexico during COVID, Russell learned of DK's fear of the water. Russell was eventually able to convince DK to get into the water, the shallow end. After a few weeks, DK was swimming around the pool in a pair of borrowed goggles. It took nearly 20 years, but he was finally able to overcome that childhood fear.

When DK was 10, his father's football career took the family back to Mississippi. They went back to their roots and ended up back in Oxford. Terrence was near the end of his career and caught on as a practice squad player for the New Orleans Saints.

Now a little older, father and son could continue their workout routine that they had started when DK was only five. This time, they added running into the mix. Father and son would run the steps together at Vaught-Hemingway Stadium, home to the Ole Miss Rebels, where Terrence played his college ball.

After the steps would come a series of 110-yard sprints. Despite being well over 300 pounds, Terrence always beat his son in the sprints. DK would sometimes fake an asthma attack to try to get his father to slow down a little. Terrence never did.

Eventually, though, the lanky DK did get the better of his father in the sprints. DK had grown and his father had slowed with time. When DK was in seventh grade, he finally beat his father in the sprints.

"As it progressed, he just started outrunning me and outworking me," Terrence said. "As much as I pushed him, it got to the point where he was competing against me to prove to me that I was never going to be able to be faster than him again or run longer than him. I just saw that shift and saw just how hard he started working."[ii]

Despite having a family pedigree and a sculpted body, Terrence would not allow DK to start playing football until he turned 12. Terrence was worried that his son wouldn't be coached properly and that it would turn him away from the game.

Then DK started to play football, and he was hooked. Football would not be his only passion, though. He also played basketball, ran track, and there was always weight lifting.

Oxford High School

By the time DK enrolled at Oxford High School, he had the height but was still lacking the powerful physique that he would become known for. That's where Jason Russell came in. Russell happened to be the strength and conditioning coach at Oxford High School. Oxford also happened to have one of the best powerlifting teams in the state of Mississippi.

Russell crafted a workout for young DK that required him to be in the gym, lifting for two hours a day, four days a week. The results started to show almost immediately.

DK started varsity as a freshman, playing both safety and wide receiver. He ended the season with 21 receptions for 360 yards and 5 touchdowns on a team that went 11-2, losing in the state quarterfinals.

After football season, DK went right into basketball season and followed that up with track. All the while, he continued with his four-day-a-week workout that Russell created for him. There were no off days for DK Metcalf.

"He never had an offseason, so he would come in before school, sometimes as early as 6 a.m., and train on his own when he was in season to make sure he was doing what he needed to do to be where he needed to be physically," said Oxford head football coach Chris Cutcliffe, who was DK's position coach at the time. "There's not many high school athletes that are willing to work like he worked."[ii]

DK excelled on the basketball court as well as in track. By his senior season, he was averaging 13 points and 7 rebounds a game for Oxford High School. In track, he set the school record in the triple jump. But it was football that kept his attention. DK finished his sophomore season with 52 receptions for 618 yards and 8 touchdowns.

Oxford went undefeated in the regular season and made it all the way to the Mississippi 5A State Championship game for the first time in school history. The Chargers had a 35-21 lead heading into the fourth quarter, and it appeared as though they were about to win their first state title. But Picayune scored 21 unanswered in the fourth quarter, including a 75-yard touchdown run with two minutes remaining to take the game. Oxford finished the year 14-1 and ranked second in the state.

It was during this season that Terrence saw something special in his son, something that he hadn't noticed before.

"He was playing against my home team back in high school at Clarksdale, and he was taking the kid, he was blocking the DB, and he took the DB all the way off the field and slammed the guy onto the track," Terrence said. "And it was in between the whistles and I just saw him do that and turn around and jog back. But his blocks in that game and from that moment on was always elbows in, hands inside, he tried to finish guys like he was an offensive lineman."[iv]

By his junior season, DK was starting to get looks from colleges across the country. Both Auburn and UCLA were chasing after the four-star recruit but there was one team that had an advantage. Ole Miss was right in DK's backyard, and his father had attended the school a few years earlier. DK was also old enough when his father was there that he remembered being on campus with Terrence.

DK's game took off during his junior season. He caught 79 passes for 1,229 yards and 19 touchdowns. Once again, Oxford made it all the way to the 5A State Championship game against Laurel. Laurel came into the game undefeated, and Oxford was 13-1, losing to another state champion, Starkville.

The Chargers found themselves down by three with 27 seconds left with the ball on Laurel's 26-yard line. On first down, Oxford's quarterback tried to hit DK in the end zone but the play was broken up at the last second. With no timeouts left, an Oxford receiver was tackled in bounds on the next play and time ran out. For the second straight year, Oxford lost in the state championship game.

In the summer before his senior season, DK's weightlifting peaked. He could squat 500 pounds, bench 295, and deadlift 595. Those numbers would be outstanding for a future FCS offensive lineman, but for a receiver, it was out of this world. For Russell, there was one moment in particular that stuck out to him. DK deadlifted 495 pounds five times in front of his entire team.

"That one just always stuck out in my head because you're looking at five plates on each side, picking it up five different times in a row, and you've got your linemen and your linebackers doing the same thing and struggling to get it, and here comes the receiver snapping out five reps, no problem," Russell said. "You don't see too many 6'4" guys being competitive in powerlifting, but he's one of those guys that if he wanted to and wasn't playing basketball, he could have come powerlift with us and have been successful in that, too."[ii]

Even DK's father was impressed with his son's ability and work ethic. More importantly, the way that DK kept challenging himself to get better every day.

"When you develop that mentality at the skill position, you can change a locker room," Terrence said. "You can change a mentality of an individual who didn't lift as much in college or high school to when they get to the NFL and they see how you work; you know you can change the mindset of an individual. And that's what I love about him. That's when I knew in high school, just with his work ethics and his mindset on the football field, when you know how to turn it on, on the field and then be who you are off the field, you know you've got a special individual that has his goals and his mind set on something."[iv]

DK had also reached another personal milestone. He was the number-one recruit in the state of Mississippi, just like his father before him. The Metcalfs were also the second father/son duo to receive a Dandy Dozen nod. The Dandy Dozen are selected by the *Clarion Ledger* and are the best 12 high school football players in the state of Mississippi. The only other players to accomplish that feat were Steve McNair and his son, Steve McNair Jr.

Just before his senior year started, DK followed in his father's footsteps once again. He made the decision to sign with Ole Miss.

"It was a blessing because it was something that I'd done," Terrence said. "To see him walking the same walk is special, and I'd be a fool to say I wasn't excited for him to commit to Ole Miss. Other schools are going to come and recruit you, but I was very excited to see that Ole Miss offered him and he wanted to play there."[iii]

There was another change for DK heading into his senior season; his father was now an assistant coach on Oxford's staff. Terrence had always been around the team since DK started playing, and he acted as an unofficial mentor to a number of the players, especially the offensive linemen. But now he would be a full-time assistant for DK's senior season.

"He motivates our guys to keep working hard," Oxford quarterback Jack Abraham said of Terrence. "Maybe we didn't have that sort of motivation last year. He works our guys really hard."[iii]

DK posted monster numbers in his senior season. He caught 93 passes for 1,455 yards and 22 touchdowns. And once again, the Chargers found themselves back in the state championship game.

With eight minutes remaining in the game, DK caught a touchdown pass that put Oxford up 41-31. He had another great game, catching 11 passes for 148 yards and two touchdowns. It looked like the Chargers were about to get their first state title. But Wayne Country scored the game's final 14 points, including a touchdown, with a little over a minute remaining in the game. For the third straight season, Oxford lost in the

Mississippi state championship game. The Chargers lost those three games by a combined 14 points.

In his four seasons with Oxford, DK caught 245 passes for 3,662 yards and 54 touchdowns. He would now be moving a few miles away to play for the Rebels, but he always took the lessons from his father with him.

"It's like cheating," DK said. "He (Terrence) knows what it takes to get there. He just stays on my back about working hard, being a leader and not a follower.[iii]

So, DK Metcalf would follow in his father's footsteps. He was headed to Ole Miss.

Chapter 2: College Career

The Rebels

The University of Mississippi is probably more well-known for what it did poorly rather than what it did well. The school and the football team were some of the last in the nation to fully integrate, and in the case of the school, were forced to do so by the government.

Ole Miss became known as the Rebels in 1936, but the name dates back to the school's Civil War roots. As the story goes, the entire class of 1862 volunteered to fight for the Confederacy. Nearly all of them were killed at Gettysburg. Hence the choice of name.

In 1962, the Ole Miss football team went undefeated as the campus exploded. Student James Meredith tried to become the first African American to enroll at the university. It would be the first and only time Ole Miss would go undefeated. Beyond that controversy, Ole Miss is best known as the school that produced Eli and Archie Manning.

In Metcalf's first game with the Rebels, he caught one pass, but it was for a three-yard touchdown in an opening-season loss against Florida State.

In his second career game, Metcalf caught a 10-yard touchdown pass in the second quarter against FCS school Wofford. Metcalf came down wrong on his foot and stayed down on the field. He was able to limp off the field and headed to the locker room. It was later revealed that Metcalf broke his foot and would be out for the remainder of his freshman season. His first year ended with two catches for 13 yards and 2 touchdowns.

"We'll do it with other guys, but obviously DK is really good at it," Ole Miss offensive coordinator Dan Werner said. "That's a tough one."[v]

And just like that, Metcalf's freshman season was over.

In the offseason, Ole Miss Head Coach Hugh Freeze resigned under a cloud of controversy. The NCAA had been investigating Freeze and the Ole Miss football program and found that the program had given athletes money and had other students take the ACT for football players. Freeze was also accused of using a university phone to call a prostitute on several occasions. The NCAA ruled that the Rebels would be ineligible for postseason play in 2017 and would also have a reduction in scholarships.

Matt Luke took over as the interim head coach for the Rebels. But none of this directly affected Metcalf as he rehabbed from his injured foot.

In his first game back, Metcalf caught eight passes for 84 yards in a win over South Alabama. The following week, he caught his first touchdown pass of the season in a win over FCS school Tennessee-Martin.

Ole Miss followed up its first two victories with three-straight road games against FCS schools, including a trip to No. 1 Alabama and No. 12 Auburn. In the first game against Cal, Metcalf had a career-high 125 yards and a touchdown in a loss.

The Rebels then suffered two blowout losses in the state of Alabama. Ole Miss was outscored 110-26 in those two losses. Metcalf had a career-high two touchdowns against Auburn, but it wasn't nearly enough, as the defense gave up 44 points.

After a win over Vanderbilt, Ole Miss dropped back-to-back games to LSU and Arkansas. Metcalf only had five catches in the two games. Against Arkansas, the Rebels had a 24-point lead in the second quarter, but the Razorbacks rallied to win the game on a last-second field goal.

The following week, the Rebels traveled to Kentucky. The game went back and forth throughout. Late in the third quarter, Metcalf caught a 58-yard touchdown pass from Jordan Ta'amu to tie the game at 27.

Kentucky scored a touchdown with a little over two minutes remaining to take a 34-30 lead. Ta'amu led the Rebels down the field and they had the ball deep in Kentucky's territory with less than 10 seconds left. Ta'amu lofted a pass in the back of the end zone toward Metcalf. He leapt in the air and came down with the game-winning touchdown with five seconds remaining.

"Jordan put it on the money," Metcalf said of the 7-yard TD with 5 seconds remaining, upheld on review, that pushed Mississippi past Kentucky for a wild 37-34 victory on Saturday. "It was just up to me to turn around and make the play."[vi]

Mississippi split games with UL-Lafayette and Texas A&M and was sitting at 5-6 heading into their rivalry game against Mississippi State. The Bulldogs were the 16th-ranked team in the country and headed to a bowl game. No matter how Ole Miss finished the year, this would be their final game, as they were ineligible for a bowl game because of an NCAA infraction.

With two minutes left in the third quarter, Metcalf caught a 63-yard touchdown pass from Ta'amu to put Ole Miss up 24-6. Mississippi State desperately tried to come back in the fourth quarter but the Rebels won the Egg Bowl, 31-28.

For a team that wasn't going to a bowl game, this was their biggest win of the season. Metcalf finished his redshirt freshman year with 39 receptions for 646 yards and 7 touchdowns.

Neck Injury

Entering the 2018 season, the Ole Miss wide receiver corps was stacked. Besides Metcalf, the team also had future NFL players A.J. Brown and Elijah Moore. Meanwhile, Jordan Ta'amu was back at quarterback, and the offensive line was anchored by Greg Little.

The Rebels opened the season with a 47-27 win over Texas Tech and followed that up with a 76-41 win over Southern Illinois. Week 3 brought Ole Miss's first true test of the season, hosting No. 1 Alabama.

Metcalf caught two passes for 92 yards and a touchdown, but Alabama throttled the Rebels 62-7. In two seasons, Ole Miss gave up 128 points to the Crimson Tide. Despite starting the season 2-1, the Ole Miss defense was giving up 43 points a game.

Ole Miss bounced back with a win over Kent State but then fell to fifth-ranked LSU, 45-16. After putting up 70 points against UL-Monroe, the Rebels traveled to War Memorial Stadium to take on Arkansas.

Six games into the season, Metcalf was on pace to eclipse all his numbers from the previous season. He already had five touchdown receptions and more than 500 yards in six games.

After catching one ball for 49 yards against Arkansas, Metcalf was blocking on a kickoff return. It was a rainy, muddy day at War Memorial. Terrence and Tonya Metcalf made the trip to Arkansas for the game, but when they looked up, DK Metcalf was lying on the ground, motionless.

"We didn't see it happen. We just kept wondering like, 'Where is DeKaylin [DK]?' And then my friends started texting me that they saw him walking in the tunnel," Tonya Metcalf said.[ii]

When she was finally able to get in touch with DK, he told her that it was just a stinger. As he was blocking, Metcalf took a shot from an opposing helmet just under his chin. His head whipped backward, twisting his neck past his shoulder. A pain shot down his left arm and brought him to his knees.

When the team returned to Oxford the following day, Metcalf went to a local hospital for a CT scan. He waited for a call from the team's trainer to give him the results. He wasn't expecting the call until Monday, but the trainer almost immediately called him and told Metcalf to get to the hospital immediately.

It wasn't a stinger. Metcalf had broken his neck. The hit created a pepper grinder action at the top of his spine. That chipped a piece of his C4 vertebra, which was sitting on a shoulder nerve, millimeters from his spine.

"That's when the doctor was like, 'You may not be able to play again. Football should be the last thing on your mind, and you need to have surgery,'" Metcalf said. "He said if I had gotten hit any harder, the bone would've pierced my spinal cord and I would have been paralyzed."[i]

Metcalf sat alone in the hospital waiting room, contemplating the end of his football career. He called his mother, who was driving home from Arkansas, to deliver the news to her.

"Outside of football, I'm looking at my child, how he could have been in a hospital bed in our living room for the rest of his life," Tonya Metcalf said. "We get there, rush to the back, and I just hugged him. I told him, 'Son, it's OK, people break their necks all the time and come back.'"[i]

Metcalf now had to consider what a life without football was going to be like for him. He seriously thought about going to culinary school. But he also went for a second opinion. The doctor determined that after surgery and months of rehab, Metcalf would be able to return to the football field.

While Metcalf had surgery, the Rebels lost their final five games without him to finish the season at 5-7.

DK's surgery was successful, and when he woke up, both of his parents were there waiting for him. His father told him, "Nothing nobody tells you determines your end. It's all about what you do when you get up out of his bed."[i]

Metcalf spent the next month sitting in a chair, wearing his neck brace. He was unable to run and could not turn his head. But he was determined not to give up on his dream.

"I found myself, my real calling in life, while I was sitting at home for a month and a half in a neck brace and in a recliner," Metcalf said. "I told myself 'Remember these days, because these days are going to make you who you are.' It shaped me into the person I am today, just being at home, thinking about life, thinking about what I want to look like in five months or 10 years down the road."[i]

Three months after surgery, Metcalf was allowed to start training again. But now, he had a decision to make. In three seasons at Ole Miss, Metcalf had missed more than a full season due to injuries. He only played in two games his freshman season before he broke his foot, and he only played in seven games his senior season before breaking his neck.

Metcalf was eligible for the NFL draft but did not have much tape for NFL scouts to look at, and that could be a double-edged sword. On one hand, there wasn't enough tape out there to start to pick apart his game; on the other hand, there was very little known about him as a player. In the end, Metcalf and his family made the decision that he would forgo his final years at Ole Miss and enter the NFL draft.

"I have enjoyed my time at Ole Miss, gaining brothers and a family, now it's time for me to pursue my dreams of playing in the NFL," Metcalf said via Twitter. "I want to thank the University, my coaches, and teammates, but most importantly my family for helping me through this process."[vii]

NFL Draft

It turned out that breaking a bone in his neck actually ended up helping DK Metcalf's draft stock. Most NFL prospects do not start training for the draft until after the bowl season ends. But once Metcalf's season ended in October and he recovered from surgery, he immediately went to work out.

Metcalf headed out to the EXOS training facility in Arizona. EXOS was a place where many NFL prospects went to train prior to the draft. Metcalf spent 12 weeks training for the draft. His trainer, Nic Hill, started with a simple change to Metcalf's lifestyle. He cut strawberry milk out of Metcalf's diet and replaced it with vegetables.

Despite not having trained in months, Metcalf was still in great physical shape. Hill described his training as "fine tuning a Ferrari engine."

"He deserves all the press that he's getting because he is such an impressive athlete just naturally, but at the same time, he works harder than maybe anybody I've worked with," said Hill. "You get a strong work ethic, and then you get a genetic monster; you put those two together and you get something special."[ii]

The results were immediate. Metcalf's body fat went from just above five percent to two percent. His shirtless photos started making the rounds online as NFL scouts marveled at how someone so big could be so fast. One scout joked that he was so big that he should be listed as the draft's top receiver, tight end, linebacker, defensive end, and safety.

But despite all the accolades that he was garnering for his incredible physique, scouts still had their doubts about him. They were concerned that he was just a workout warrior and that he couldn't stay on the field. Out of a possible 36 games at Ole Miss, Metcalf had only played in 21 of them.

Only being a redshirt sophomore was another disadvantage for Metcalf. He was not invited to play in any of the postseason showcase games. This meant that there was immense pressure for him to perform well at the NFL Combine. It would be his only opportunity to impress NFL teams.

At the NFL Combine, there is the seen and unseen. The seen is the quantifiable results. The numbers tell a story of how strong or fast a particular player is. Players can rise up draft boards solely based on their numbers. Then, there is the unseen. The interviews that the players have with teams can tell an entirely different story.

Sometimes teams will pass on a particular player, and no one can really understand why. What the team learned in the interview may have dissuaded them from picking a particular player. However, if the interview goes well, the team will know that a player is a perfect fit for their team. In the interview, anything can happen.

When Metcalf sat down with the Seahawks, a Seattle scout asked him to rip his shirt off before sitting down with Seahawks head coach Pete Carroll. Metcalf agreed to rip his shirt off. Without thinking about it, Carroll, who was in his 60s at the time, ripped his shirt off too.

"A scary sight," Metcalf said. "He missed a few ab days, in my opinion. But he showed the type of person he was and the type of coach he was. It was a calming moment. The meeting went very well."[i]

And then DK started working out. He benched 225 pounds 27 times, tied for the most by any receiver at the combine. He then went out and ran the 40-yard dash in 4.33 seconds, the second-fastest time for a receiver. Everyone was impressed.

"We had a guy walk in our room last night, a receiver out of Ole Miss. His name is Metcalf, and he looked like Jim Brown," Raiders head coach Jon Gruden said. "I mean, he's the biggest wideout I've ever seen, and you've got to ask yourself, 'Who's tackling this guy?'"[ii]

But DK did not do quite as well in the cone drill and the shuttle run. In fact, his times were worse than the notoriously terrible times turned in by Tom Brady. Some scouts began to worry that he might be too stiff and that he would be too slow out of his break.

Despite what other people said about him, Metcalf was proud of his performance. After his neck injury and recovery, he honestly was just thrilled that he was able to run again. Once he finished his 40-yard dash, he immediately called his mother.

"He had called and he was crying," Tonya Metcalf said. "We told him we're proud of him. That's all I was saying to him on the phone. We weren't surprised by what he had done because we knew how hard he had worked. And to everything he was like, 'Yes, ma'am, yes ma'am.'"[ii]

But it was more than that. It was a lifetime of work and a family that was there to support him the entire way.

"Just going back to how many times I had to call my mom because I left something for practice, or my dad being there, my dad driving four hours from Pearl River just to come to my games on Saturday," Metcalf said. "It just means a lot and just all that they went through just for these moments, for that moment, just for me to perform at my best. On draft night, it's going to be that much sweeter because of all the hard work that we put in just to get to this moment."[ii]

Based on his combine performance, Metcalf was invited to attend the first round of the draft in

Nashville. He would be there with all the other picks waiting for their names to be called.

But as the draft progressed, DK did not hear his name called. In between picks, the camera would flash to the handful of players still waiting to be picked. After the first 20 picks, it starts to get embarrassing. Stories of Aaron Rodgers waiting in the green room then start to circulate on television.

It wasn't just Metcalf, however; there were no receivers selected in the first 20 picks of the draft. Finally, at 25, the Ravens took Marquise Brown out of Oklahoma. Then, with the final pick in the first round, the Patriots selected receiver N'Keal Harry out of Arizona State.

Two receivers had been selected ahead of him. The Metcalf family got in their car and drove home to Oxford that night. No one spoke.

As the second round started, more receivers started hearing their names called. The 49ers took Deebo

Samuel out of South Carolina, and the Titans selected Metcalf's college teammate, A.J. Brown. Three more receivers were taken after Brown. Combined, those three did not have as many receptions as Metcalf.

Two picks before the end of the second round, the Cardinals took receiver Andy Isabella out of UMASS. He was the only receiver to run a 40-yard dash faster than Metcalf. He has 33 career receptions.

Finally, with the final pick in the second round, the Seattle Seahawks selected DK Metcalf out of Mississippi.

When Metcalf got the call from Coach Carroll, he asked him, "Why'd y'all wait so long, man?"

Metcalf was now taking his skills from Oxford, Mississippi, to Seattle, Washington.

Chapter 3: Pro Career

Rookie Year

The 2019 Seattle Seahawks were a team in transition. The "Legion of Boom," led by cornerback Richard Sherman and safety Earl Thomas, was gone. It had been five years since the Seahawks had been to the Super Bowl, where they had lost to the Patriots on one of the most controversial calls in the history of the game.

Seattle was down by four late in the game. They had the ball deep in New England territory. Instead of running the ball with Marshawn Lynch, which most people believed was their best chance, a pass play was called instead. Russell Wilson was subsequently picked off and the Patriots won the game.

Now, the team turned to its quarterback Russell Wilson. Wilson was drafted in the third round out of Wisconsin. He was supposed to be the backup to newly-signed starter Matt Flynn, but during training camp, Wilson was able to win the job.

When Metcalf arrived, Wilson had been in Seattle for seven seasons. Rather than ignore his new second-round target, Wilson and Metcalf started getting together before the season to learn more about each other. Like any good quarterback-receiver team, it's important to know each other's likes/dislikes and tendencies. You learn about each other during the offseason so that when the cameras are on during the season, you already know what the other person is going to do.

In his first career game, DK Metcalf showed the NFL what he could do. He caught four passes for 89 yards, setting the Seahawks' record for most yards for a rookie in his first start. He broke the record formerly held by Hall-of-Famer Seahawk Steve Largent.

Seattle held on for a 21-20 victory. Wilson threw a 44-yard touchdown early in the fourth quarter that proved to be the game-winning score.

In Week 2, Seattle traveled across the country to take on the Pittsburgh Steelers. The Steelers took a 10-7 lead into the half, but Seattle came storming back in the third quarter to take a 21-13 lead. After a Pittsburgh touchdown, Wilson hit Metcalf for a 28-yard touchdown catch. It was his first career touchdown reception, and it proved to be the game-winning touchdown as well, as Seattle held on to win the game 28-26.

After a loss to New Orleans and a win over Arizona, Seattle next hosted the LA Rams. The Rams had turned themselves into Seattle's primary rival in the NFC West. LA had just lost the Super Bowl to the Patriots the previous season. They had one of the best young coaches in the NFL in Sean McVay, and the best defensive player in the league in Aaron Donald.

In the second quarter, Wilson hit Metcalf on a 40-yard touchdown catch to put Seattle up 14-6. Wilson put up career numbers in the game, throwing four touchdowns, including the game-winner, with just over two minutes remaining. Metcalf only caught one other pass in the game for four yards.

After eight games, Seattle found themselves at 6-2 and sitting in second place in the NFC West. Their rivals, San Francisco, were still undefeated. Metcalf had four touchdown catches, but his play was inconsistent. His first game was his best, with 89 yards. He had yet to have his break-out game. But that would come in Week 9 against the Tampa Bay Buccaneers in a shootout between Wilson and former Heisman Trophy winner Jameis Winston. Wilson threw for a career-high five touchdowns, but it was Metcalf that showed his skills.

With the game tied late in the fourth quarter, Wilson hit Metcalf on a short pass and he took off. Metcalf scored on a 53-yard touchdown catch.

Tampa would come back to tie the score and send the game to overtime. In overtime, Metcalf caught a 29-yard pass that moved the ball inside the Tampa 10-yard line. Seattle would score the game-winning touchdown on the next play.

For Metcalf, it was his best game as a pro. He caught 6 passes for 123 yards and a touchdown.

"He's trusting me. It starts in practice. He's trusting me in practice and it translates to the game," Metcalf said of Wilson after the game.[viii]

The following week, Seattle knocked off the undefeated San Francisco 49ers in overtime. It was Seattle's third straight win. The Seahawks would go on to win five straight before losing a game to the Rams.

Seattle struggled after that, ending the season losing three of four games, and finishing the year at 11-5, which was good enough to secure a Wild Card berth in the playoffs.

DK Metcalf ended his rookie season with 58 catches for exactly 900 yards and 7 touchdowns. He did not receive a single vote for Offensive Rookie of the Year, but his college teammate, A.J. Brown, received votes. However, he lost to Raiders running back Josh Jacobs.

Seattle opened the playoffs at Philadelphia. The Eagles and DK Metcalf had some unfinished business going back to the draft. As the second round of the draft started to get toward its completion, the Eagles had been on the clock with the 57th pick. Philadelphia needed a receiver, and their decision came down to two possible selections: Metcalf or J.J. Arcega-Whiteside. The Eagles took Arcega-Whiteside, and Metcalf continued his slide down the draft board.

"We liked the player," Eagles Coach Doug Pederson said. "He's a big, powerful, physical guy, and he had some really good tape out there. And then we also liked J.J. We loved his size, his ability to play above the rim so to speak in the red zone and things like that. Similar players and made the decision with J.J. and we've been happy with that."[ix]

Metcalf had a great rookie season, while Arcega-Whiteside barely played for the Eagles. After the 2021 season, Arcega-Whiteside was out of the league with 16 career receptions. But despite having a better rookie season, Metcalf still carried a bit of a grudge into the playoff game against Philly.

Early in the game, the Seattle defense knocked Philadelphia quarterback Carson Wentz out of the game. The Eagles never really got any offense going without their quarterback. But the story of the game would be DK Metcalf. In the third quarter, Philadelphia got within a touchdown, but then Wilson hit Metcalf for a 53-yard touchdown to put Seattle up for good.

"I caught the ball, I didn't feel anybody touch me," Metcalf said. "I got back up and I wanted a touchdown. I wanted a touchdown, real bad."[x]

In total, Metcalf caught seven passes for 160 yards. He set a new NFL record for most receiving yards by a rookie in a playoff game.

The following week, the Seahawks took on the Packers in the NFC Divisional Round. Throughout the game, Wilson was constantly harassed by the Green Bay defense. He was sacked five times in the game.

The Packers took a 21-3 halftime lead, but the Seahawks fought their way back into the game. Seattle got the ball back, down 28-23 with two minutes remaining. But Wilson was sacked again, and it ended any chance of the Seahawks winning the game. Their season ended with a 28-23 loss. Metcalf caught four passes for 59 yards in the losing effort. It was a sad ending to what had been a solid opening season for the second-round draft pick.

COVID Season

When the COVID-19 pandemic hit, it appeared as though there was not going to be an NFL season. It made for some strange changes to the offseason program for Metcalf and Wilson. Usually, the two would travel around the country, meeting up with other receivers and working on their game. But none of that would work during COVID.

Wilson was essentially trapped in Mexico. His wife, Ciara, was pregnant and did not feel safe traveling. So, Metcalf packed his bags and headed to their private offseason hangout in Southern Baja, Mexico.

It was the first time that DK had ever left the country. But he remembered there were a few necessities that he was going to need for a visit with Wilson. Metcalf made sure to bring his cleats and his helmet.

"We're both trying to figure out what greatness looks like," Wilson said of their offseason in Mexico.[i]

The two found a soccer field nearby and worked on their skills every day. Ciara even came out to film the training sessions. But these workouts became about more than just working on skills; it was about anticipating what the other was going to do. Day after day, Wilson and Metcalf worked on different scenarios and routes. Metcalf began to expand his route tree from the original three that he came into the league with to dozens. He was slowly becoming an all-around receiver.

"There's a whole other level of the game that we thought we could really go to, me and him," Wilson said. "We want to make it one of those special Joe Montana-Jerry Rice type relationships. We've spent a lot of one-on-one time just putting the extra work in, and it's definitely shown up in so many different ways so far."[i]

There was more than just football going on in Mexico. The two were building friendship and trust, as they had all their meals together and played golf. Through that trust, Metcalf revealed to Wilson that he did not know how to swim. He told him about how his mom had once signed him up for swim lessons when he was four; he jumped in the pool and never resurfaced. His instructor finally had to fish him out of the pool. He never went back near a pool since that incident.

Now, with his quarterback, Metcalf decided it might be time to get in again. Wilson was able to convince him to get into the shallow end. Metcalf borrowed a pair of goggles, and all six foot, four inches of him stood in the shallow end. Eventually, Metcalf put his face in the water and started blowing bubbles.

Once Metcalf was able to relax, he was able to start swimming up and down the pool. His trust in Wilson got him over his initial fear of the water.

"In a couple of years, I'll be looking to take down Michael Phelps," Metcalf joked.[i]

When the duo returned to America for camp, there were some changes in Seattle. One of the new faces in Seattle camp was tight end Greg Olsen. Olsen had an odd history with the Metcalf family, perhaps the only time that this has happened in NFL history. Olsen was once a rookie with the Chicago Bears and played with DK Metcalf's father, Terrence.

"It was one day, like a month ago. Me and Greg worked out and I brought my dad up there with me, and they rekindled an old flame," Metcalf said. "They just started smiling and Greg was like, 'Oh I gotta tell you about some stories in the locker room.' It looked like they had a pretty good relationship. Me just learning from Greg has been great. He's been teaching me a lot this offseason, since he's been in the league 20 years. He's a great player and tight end just to learn from him is going to be special this year."[xi]

Olsen had not really been in the league for 20 years—it was just Metcalf having some fun with him. But the two started building not just a relationship but a mutual respect.

"He's a special type of player," Olsen said of Metcalf. "And there's so much room for growth. He's probably just scratching the surface, and that's a scary thought."[i]

Metcalf started to build relationships with everyone on the team. He was no longer a rookie and wanted to make an impression on everyone. Every Tuesday morning, he and veteran linebacker Bobby Wagner started a routine. They would start at 7 a.m. by working out, then breaking down game films. Tuesday is usually an off-day for players, but these two would spend their days talking football and then anything else that Metcalf wanted to learn from the five-time Pro Bowler.

"We talk about life stuff," Metcalf said. "He talks about books that he wants me to read, that I've yet to read. He talks about how he takes care of his family and how he's saved his money. Pretty much just Life Lessons from Bobby."[i]

In Week 1, Metcalf's offseason work was on display for the entire country. He caught 4 passes for 95 yards and a touchdown in a blowout win over Atlanta.

Week 2 presented a unique challenge for Metcalf. The Seahawks were taking on the New England Patriots and All-Pro cornerback Stephon Gilmore. On the first play of the game, Metcalf blasted off the line and started blocking Gilmore. He nearly pushed the smaller cornerback off the field.

"I knew I was going to try to drive his head into the ground," Metcalf said. "It always goes back to being a dog, to bring that mentality out of the receiving position: a street fight every time you line up."[i]

Metcalf caught a 54-yard touchdown pass in the second quarter to tie the score at 14. He ended the game with four catches for 92 yards against the league's best corner. But it was Seattle's defense that was the star of the game. They were able to stuff New England's quarterback Cam Newton on a quarterback sneak from one yard out to end the game. The Seahawks won the game to start the season 2-0.

In Week 3 against Dallas, DK Metcalf reminded everyone that he was still young but still very good. In the first quarter, he broke away for a long gain that appeared to be an easy touchdown. However, he started his celebration a little early and Dallas cornerback Trevon Diggs knocked the ball loose for a touchback.

But later in the game, DK was able to redeem himself. With the game tied with less than two minutes to go, Metcalf caught a 29-yard touchdown pass from Wilson to win the game. The mistake was forgiven and his game-winning catch became the story.

"The lesson learned will help everybody and fortunately we overcame it and didn't wreck the game for us," Seattle Coach Pete Carroll said. "But it's a terrible play. It really is because he's got a touchdown, just finish it off, and he started celebrating too early."xii

After a win over Miami, the Seahawks hosted the Vikings. Seattle found itself down 26-21 with 1:21 left to play. The Seahawks were facing a fourth and 10 from their own 23. Wilson was able to find Metcalf for a 39-yard reception to keep the game going. Wilson then went back to Metcalf in the end zone for a six-yard touchdown that won the game for the Seahawks 27-26.

"I had 100 percent feeling he was going to throw the ball to me," Metcalf said. "It was just going to come down to: Am I going to let the ball just fall into my hands or am I going to go attack the ball and be better than last year? Because last year I would just let the ball fall into my arms and not go attack it. So I would say that's a year of growth, of him trusting me more in that situation. And it all comes from the practices and the workouts in Mexico."[i]

It was the first time in the history of the Seattle Seahawks that the team started a season 5-0. That streak came to an end on Week 6 as the Seahawks dropped their first game of the season to the Cardinals, but that is not what people will remember. DK Metcalf only caught two passes for 23, but that will soon be forgotten, too. What people will remember is Metcalf's only tackle in the game.

The Seahawks had the ball deep in Arizona territory. Wilson dropped back to throw and the ball floated on him. Metcalf was running a shallow crossing route just across the end line. Arizona safety Budda Baker broke on the ball and intercepted the pass. When Baker looked up, there was nothing in front of him except grass, so he took off toward the opposing end zone.

Meanwhile, Metcalf planted his feet at the two-yard line, with Baker a good 10 yards in front of him. Metcalf mumbled to himself, "All right, go get him."

By the time Baker hit the 50-yard line, every other player on the Seahawks had given up on the tackle, but not DK. He kicked it into another gear and went after Baker. Just before Baker scored, Metcalf got his man, taking him down short of the touchdown.

After the game, Seahawks Coach Pete Carroll called it "the play of the Century." Despite the loss, Metcalf still made his mark—and dozens of memes!

Metcalf and the Seahawks bounced back the following week with a win over the 49ers. Metcalf had the best game of his career up to that point, notching a career-high 12 receptions for a career-high 161 yards and a career-high 2 touchdowns.

Next, the Seahawks dropped two straight to the Bills and Rams, but bounced back with a win over the Cardinals. But then the Seahawks had to play the

Eagles. And no team brought the best out of Metcalf like the Philadelphia Eagles. DK had the rookie receiving playoff record the previous season against the team that had passed on him in the draft.

To show the Eagles just how good he was, Metcalf set a new career-high with 177 yards receiving in a 23-17 win over Philadelphia.

"I'm getting a little respect, but you know I still got work to do. One of the defensive coaches came up to me and it kind of made me mad that he was like, 'You know, I was in Detroit with Megatron but you're not there yet,'" Metcalf said. "In my mind, I'm not trying to be Megatron. I'm trying to be me. So I had a little chip on my shoulder the whole game."[xiii]

If the Eagles learned nothing else from playing against Metcalf, they should at least know not to say anything to put another chip on his shoulder.

After a home loss to the Giants, the Seahawks won four straight in convincing fashion to end the season at

12-4. Metcalf ended the year with 83 receptions for 1,303 yards and 10 touchdowns. He was named to the Pro Bowl for the first time in his career and was second team All-Pro.

The Seahawks hosted division rival Rams in the Wild Card Round of the NFL Playoffs. Two weeks earlier, the Seahawks had beaten the Rams to clinch the NFC West and were seen smoking victory cigars on the sideline before the game ended. That did not sit well with the Rams.

Cam Akers ran all over the Seahawks' defense, and despite Metcalf's best efforts, Seattle was still blown out in the game.

"We come up here, and all week we were told how good they are and how we snuck into the playoffs," Rams quarterback Jared Goff said. "Two weeks ago you saw them smoking cigars and getting all excited about beating us, and winning the division, and we were able to come up here and beat them."[xiv]

Metcalf ended the game with 5 catches for 96 yards and 2 touchdowns. In three career playoff games, Metcalf had 16 catches for 315 yards and 3 touchdowns.

Losing

In 2020, DK Metcalf established himself as one of the best receivers in the NFL. But around him, the Seahawks were dramatically changing. Linebacker K.J. Wright left the team after the 2020 season. He had been with the Seahawks since the 2010 season.

Furthermore, the Seahawks did not have a first-round draft pick after trading it to the Jets for safety Jamal Adams. But Adams spent most of his time injured. With the loss of Wright, the Seattle defense was starting to lose its identity. That identity had led the team to two Super Bowls, and now, the team was rapidly losing all those players.

While all these changes were taking place in Seattle, Metcalf was busy trying something. Just prior to the

COVID season, the 2020 Olympic Games in Tokyo were postponed. With the athletes unable to train for the games and travel in Japan restricted, the organizers had no choice but to put the games off for one year.

With the additional year, this gave Metcalf time to train for an opportunity at the Olympics. When he was in high school, Metcalf was on the track and field team, and he was a part of the State Championship winning 4X100 relay team that set the Mississippi state record.

But training to go against Olympic caliber sprinters was vastly different than facing off against high school competition. For one thing, Metcalf was huge compared to these runners. He was nearly six inches taller and weighed 75 pounds more than the average sprinter.

In his first ever individual 100-meter race, DK more than held his own against seasoned sprinters. He finished 15th out of 18 sprinters. He was only .4

seconds behind the winner. It was a respectable showing for a first-time sprinter.

"Personally, it was a good experience," Metcalf said in a news conference after the race. "Anybody else who has a different opinion, you're entitled to your own opinion. But I think I did well for myself."[xv]

For Metcalf, this was just another way for him to train his body. He wanted to see if he had it in him, and he proved to himself that he could hang with the fastest men on Earth.

"Just another way to test my body, to test myself against different athletes, besides just doing football training all day," he said. "Just because I was out here doesn't mean I disrespect any other athlete or sport. I just respect myself and what I can do."[xv]

Since he missed out on the Olympics, it was back to the football field for Metcalf. Seattle was coming off an NFC West Championship but they were beaten down in the playoffs by the Rams.

There was some concern entering the season. The Seattle offense did not look good in the final weeks of the regular season or the Wild Card playoff game. There were also some low rumblings that the team might consider trading their Super Bowl winning quarterback, Russell Wilson.

After a Week 1 win over the Colts, the Seahawks dropped two in a row. Then, they were able to beat division rival San Francisco but then lost three in a row. Seattle had their worst start to a season in the Russell Wilson era.

Wilson and Metcalf were putting up good numbers, but the defense was giving up huge chunks of yards to the opposing teams. Even if the offense could deliver a lead, the defense gave it right back to the other team. Then, Wilson got hurt, costing him three games. Wilson fractured the middle finger on his throwing hand. The Seahawks had to turn to backup Gino Smith.

"Let's just look at what happened," Carroll told reporters. "We had Russ [Wilson] playing, then he left in the Rams game. Then we had to bounce back with Geno [Smith], which he did a nice job, but we altered what we were doing to make sure that we gave ourselves a win. Then we come back at the Packers, and it was Russell's first game back. I think we needed to settle everything down and get back to the ball that we liked earlier in the year. We thought that we started to get things rolling, but it's been tumultuous in that regard. I think not having Chris [Carson] where we were really leaning on Chris has made a difference to us, too. Those are just the situations that he has had to deal with, and it hasn't been easy. I'm looking forward, we have eight weeks to do something, so we will see where we wind up after that. We need to make progress."[xvi]

Without Wilson, now both the offense and defense were struggling. The Seahawks lost back-to-back heartbreakers to the Steelers and the Saints. Against the Steelers, the Seahawks blew a lead in the fourth quarter, and the game went to overtime.

Late in overtime, T.J. Watt sacked Geno Smith, and the ball squirted away from Smith. The Steelers recovered deep in Seahawk territory and were able to kick the game-winning field goal.

After a Metcalf touchdown catch in the first quarter, the Seahawks were only able to manage a field goal the rest of the way against the Saints. Seattle managed less than 200 yards of total offense in the game as New Orleans took the game 13-10.

It was the first three-game losing streak for the Seahawks in more than a decade, and the first time Seattle started 0-3 at home in more than 30 years. And even when Wilson came back, the Seahawks did not make much progress, losing the first three games of his return. A December loss to the Rams ended the Seahawks playoff hopes for 2021. The Rams had ended Seattle's season the previous year in the playoffs.

Metcalf did end the season with a bang. In the second-to-last game of the year, the Seahawks and the Lions had a shootout in Seattle. Metcalf set a new career-high with three touchdowns. There was a scary moment, however. With the defense on the field, Metcalf was put on the trainer's cart and taken to the locker room. There was a moment of confusion in the stadium and on the broadcast. No one had seen Metcalf get hurt.

A few minutes later, DK jogged back onto the field. He seemed to be just fine. That scare turned into a hilarious moment after the game. Metcalf revealed that he just had to use the bathroom, and he wasn't sure if he would make it to the locker room if he ran, so he got a ride. After the career game, Metcalf just tweeted out a poop emoji to let everyone know that he was fine.

It just goes to show that football players, especially Metcalf, have a pretty good sense of humor.

After the game, Wilson was the last player off the field. There were already rumblings that the Seahawks were considering shopping their franchise quarterback in the offseason, and in his final home game of the season, Wilson wanted to soak it all in.

"I was just thinking about joy and I was thinking about our fans," Wilson said. "I was thinking about just, what a special moment to be able to, you know, win this game at home for our fans and for them to feel that energy again."[xvii]

The Seahawks ended the year at 7-10. It was the first losing season since 2011 and the first losing season with Russell Wilson as the starting quarterback.

In the offseason, Metcalf had foot surgery to repair an injury that had occurred in Week 4 against the 49ers. He did not complain about the injury all year, even though he could have easily used it as an excuse for his lower production. Instead, he played through the pain and continued to get on the field every week.

"The training staff did a great job of managing me and my reps throughout the whole season, so everything worked out just fine," Metcalf said after the season ended.[xviii]

Metcalf spent six weeks in a walking boot before he could resume his off-season training program. He did manage to get back on the track again, running in the United States Track and Field Gold Games. After only a few weeks of training, DK finished dead last, but managed to lower his 100-meter time to 10.37 seconds.

After three seasons in the NFL, Metcalf became one of only eight receivers in NFL history with more than 3,000 yards and at least 29 touchdowns. It is elite company that includes Jerry Rice and Randy Moss.

Changes

Two months after the season ended, the Seattle Seahawks traded Russell Wilson to the Denver Broncos. In exchange for Wilson, Seattle received quarterback Drew Lock, tight end Noah Fant, defensive end Shelby Harris, two first-round picks, and two second-round picks.

"This has always been a challenging time of year where we have consistently maintained a competitive approach to getting better as a team," said head coach Pete Carroll. "As Jody stated, Russ' desire in doing something different afforded the organization an opportunity to compete in multiple ways. He has always been the ultimate competitor whose leadership and consistency helped shape our culture. Our franchise has won a lot of games and we will always be grateful for the exciting moments and incredible records."[xix]

But for DK Metcalf, the trading of his friend and mentor hit a little differently.

"I never thought he was gonna leave Seattle," Metcalf said about Wilson. "I was in just in shock because I didn't think it was gonna happen."[xx]

Shortly after the Seahawks traded Wilson, the team also released linebacker Bobby Wagner. Metcalf and Wagner had been meeting every Tuesday during the season to go over game film and talk about life. But now, he was on his own.

"So, my mind was like 'All right, Russ gone, what do I do?' Later that night, Bobby gets cut ... and me and Bobby—that was my guy," Metcalf said. "When he left, that hurt. That was my big brother. It's my time in Seattle, now. That's the way I look at it."[xx]

But there were also questions about Metcalf's future with the Seahawks. He was heading into the final year of his rookie contract with the team and trying to work out a new deal. But the wide receiver market exploded in the 2022 offseason. Receiver Davante Adams signed a $140-million deal with the Raiders, and Tyreek Hill signed a $120 million deal with the Dolphins. It appeared as though Metcalf was headed for a similar deal, but Seahawks' general manager John Schneider wasn't so sure.

"There's a sense of shock when you see where the numbers are going, especially at that position," Schneider said. "Everybody loves DK. He's a great player. People have to game plan for him, and he influences every single game that he's a part of, whether it's people shifting coverages his way or him just running straight through the coverage or having guys play man where he's just tossing people off him. He influences games, there's no question about it. We love him. Everybody in the building loves him. Specifically with extensions and contract situations, we don't get into that."[xx]

As training camp neared, Metcalf threatened a hold-in for training camp, meaning he would report to camp but not participate in any team activities until his contract negotiations were settled.

Just days before training camp was set to begin, Metcalf and the Seahawks reached an agreement on a three-year, $72-million extension with $58 million guaranteed.

"This means a lot to me, for my future, my family's future, my future with the Seahawks," Metcalf said after signing. "It just means a lot, and it's a blessing to get it done and behind me. I'm excited to go back to practice and rejoin the team fully. To see all my hard work and dedication pay off, it's big thanks to my parents, and all my coaches and teachers who put up with me throughout high school and college. It just means a lot, because this is their hard work too of raising me and putting up with me."[xxi]

After the ink dried on his contract, Metcalf got on the phone with his parents to let them know it was over and thank them for everything they did for him.

So, Metcalf and the Seahawks entered the 2022 season with him as the new face of the franchise. Gino Smith, who stepped in for Wilson the previous season, was now the starting quarterback in Seattle.

"I believe sitting behind Russ [Wilson] really like motivated him and really showed him how good he could really be in this league cause even at practice, he's yelling at the practice squad guys to run their routes right. He's like, 'This is my opportunity too'. And I'm like, 'Ok I respect that 'cause you understand what's at stake,'" said Metcalf. "We traded Russ and he's the starter, he comes into training camp and he's locked in, like body wise, mentally, watching the film. I saw the transition from 'Ok, I'm a backup'. To 'Ok, this is my team, I'm a starter.'"[xxii]

In the first game of the season, the NFL had some drama in mind. Seattle would host Russell Wilson and his new team, the Denver Broncos. Smith threw two touchdowns in his first game as the full-time starter.

But with less than two minutes remaining, the Broncos were down by one with the ball. It appeared to be set up for Wilson to make a comeback drive to win the game. The Broncos faced a fourth and 10 from just inside Seattle territory. Instead of going for it, Denver opted for a 64-yard game-winning field goal attempt. The attempt wasn't close, especially from that far out. Denver and Smith ended up winning the game.

"For him to go out there and get a win like that shows the confidence we have in him," Metcalf said of Smith after the game.[xxiii]

Metcalf didn't have great numbers in the game, but his team did win. Seattle dropped the next two games but beat Detroit. After a loss to New Orleans, Seattle went on a four-game winning streak. After nine games,

Seattle was a surprise 6-3. Metcalf had solid numbers, but not great. The team began relying on its running game and play-action passes.

After their winning streak, Seattle dropped five of six to go to 7-8 on the season. The Seahawks were able to take care of the lifeless Jets to improve to 8-8 on the year. A win over the Rams would put them back in the playoffs.

A year after winning the Super Bowl, the Rams were ravaged by injuries and not playing any of their superstar players in the game. Seattle managed to sneak by them 19-16 to secure a playoff berth.

Seattle would travel to San Francisco to take on the NFC West champions. In two games against the 49ers, Seattle scored a total of 20 points, and Metcalf only had 90 yards and no touchdowns.

The 49ers jumped out to an early 10-0 lead after the first quarter, but Seattle jumped back into the game in the second. Metcalf caught a 50-yard touchdown pass from Smith to put the Seahawks up 14-13 with five minutes remaining in the quarter. The teams traded field goals, but Seattle was up by a point heading into the second half.

The teams traded punts to start the third, but then San Francisco started to pour it on. In the span of 22 minutes, the 49ers scored 25 straight points to put the game out of reach. Metcalf did catch a second late touchdown, but it was too late. The 49ers won the game 41-23.

In the game, Metcalf caught 10 passes for 136 yards and 2 touchdowns. His 50-yard touchdown tied him with Randy Moss for the second-most playoff touchdown catches of 50 or more yards in NFL history. He is one behind John Stallworth for the most ever. Metcalf tied the record after only his fourth career playoff game.

"He's a fantastic player," Seahawks coach Pete Carroll said. "He's an amazing player and he just came through again. There was a lot of big strong tough-guy stuff that he did. The tough slants and getting inside of those guys when they were grabbing and clawing and all that to come through to make the catch. The deep ball was awesome. It was a great throw and catch, and great route and all of that. He was really good today."[xxiv]

After the 2022 season, Metcalf was only 25 years old. When his contract is up in Seattle, he will only be 28. The sky is the limit for the kid who once believed that he was never going to play football again.

The Seahawks resigned quarterback Geno Smith after the 2022 season to a three-year contract extension. Smith was named the Associated Press Comeback Player of the Year after leading the NFL in completion percentage. His contract runs the exact same length as Metcalf's.

"He's kept his mouth shut the past three years," Metcalf said. "Played behind Russ and when Russ went down, he stepped in and did his job. And this past season, even when they traded Russ, he didn't skip a beat with me or Tyler (Lockett). Just took the keys to the offense and ran with it."[xxv]

Metcalf and Smith found surprising success together. They were able to get to the playoffs in what at the beginning of the season seemed like a transition year for Seattle. And now, the duo has mutual respect and will be together for at least the next three seasons.

Metcalf may not have the same relationship with Smith that he had with Wilson, but that takes time. It took Metcalf time to get where he is now, and at his age, he's got plenty of that.

Besides his work on the field, Metcalf has also emerged as a leader in the Seahawks locker room. Without Wilson around, the team needed leaders and DK stepped up to fill that void.

"I will say it's more about me handling my business," said Metcalf. "Just leading by example and showing the young guys how to practice and just going hard every play I get. I'm enjoying it every chance that I get, but now I'm just in a role where I'm looking to build people up like Coby (Bryant), Tariq (Woolen), and Kenneth Walker. Just the young guys so they don't have to feel like 'Oh, I'm out here alone,' or they feel like they are far away from home and by themselves. No, we got a team and we are building a team aspect to where we are a band of brothers and we are going to fight together on Sundays and at practice and we're still going to joke and laugh around, but when it's time to get serious, it's time to get serious."[xxiv]

Even Coach Pete Carroll saw a change in his young wide receiver.

"I think he's going to lead by his work ethic and his performance that follows that," said Carroll. "I'm not asking him to make any speeches. I don't ask guys to do that. It depends on who the people are. He's such a phenomenal competitor and worker. That's how he sets the tone. And he did it again yesterday or two days ago, he had a great practice. He was battling all over the place. You can't help but elevate and try to hang with the guy. I think he's got marvelous leadership qualities, but they're going to come out in his way. He's a great worker."[xxiv]

This offseason, Metcalf has gone back to training for the Olympics. He has made it his mission to make the USA track and field team for the 2024 games in Paris. At that time, he will be 26, old for a sprinter. But despite that, Metcalf has told people in interviews that the Olympics "will happen."

And at this point in his life, who would be willing to bet against DK Metcalf? He came back from a neck injury that nearly ended his career and has not missed a single game in his entire four-year NFL career.

Chapter 4: Personal Life

DK Metcalf is not currently married. He has been linked to Instagram model Cirena Wilson, who has been seen at many of his games and lives in the Seattle area.

The Metcalf family still calls Oxford, Mississippi home. DK gets back as often as he can, but it's a long trip from Seattle. And with five other children, it is sometimes hard for Tonya and Terrence to get to games to see him.

After coaching DK during his senior season at Oxford, Terrence stayed in coaching. In 2021, he began coaching at Coahoma Community College in his hometown of Clarksdale, Mississippi. In 2022, he was named interim head coach during the season, and after the season, he was named the head coach.

DK is not the only athlete in his family. Both of his younger brothers play football, and his youngest sister, Zoe, is a budding basketball star at Oxford High

School. His cousin TJ Metcalf is also a three-star recruit at safety in Alabama.

DK has not forgotten his basketball roots. In 2023, he made the trip out to Utah to play in the NBA Celebrity All-Star Game on the Friday night of All-Star weekend. But he didn't just show up for the game—DK dominated the game. He scored 20 points, including some monster dunks, and blocked a few shots. He was named the game MVP.

While he is dominating on the basketball court, DK is also trying to prove that he is the fastest man in the NFL. While at the combine, he ran the 40-yard dash in 4.33 seconds. In fact, he has often bragged about being the fastest in the NFL. But Miami Dolphins wide receiver Tyreek Hill has challenged DK on his boast, declaring that *he* is the fastest. Tyreek called out DK and said that the two should race to determine who the fastest man in the league actually was. Despite having plenty of time to decide this, they have not been able to come up with a time or a place. But just this year, DK said that he wasn't going to race a 30-year-old man. It was a shot at Tyreek, who actually doesn't turn 30 for another year.

"Look, my people reached out to his people, just couldn't come to an agreement," Metcalf said. "I've been trying to come to an agreement for two years now. We've been trying to come to an agreement for two years. It just ain't worked out. You've seen me running in a track meet. I didn't race against no 30-year-olds, but I raced against some real track-and-field athletes. So whenever you wanna do that, hop on the track. I've got a different type of speed. I've got DK speed. He's the 'Cheetah' so he's got cheetah speed. I've got DK speed. That's just me."[xxvi]

At his fastest, Tyreek ran a 4.29 40-yard dash, but that was seven years ago. Back in 2018, Tyreek was clocked running 22.60 miles per hour. Just last year,

DK was clocked running 22.64 miles per hour in a game.

DK better be careful what he wishes for, though. Tyreek ran track in high school, but also ran at Oklahoma State, and he recently won the 60-meter indoor at the USA Track and Field Masters Indoor Championships. But the race was only for men aged 25-29.

It would be interesting to see which one of them ends up being the fastest man in the NFL. Perhaps they could get together and race for charity. Tyreek has suggested that both men put up $50,000, with all the money going to the winner's charity of choice. We'll have to see what happens.

DK does have his sights set on qualifying for the Olympics. When he was at Oxford High School in Mississippi, DK was a part of the 4X100 team that still owns the state record. After the 2020 Olympics in

Tokyo were postponed due to COVID, DK had his shot.

He finished ninth in the US qualifiers in the 100 meters. His time of 10.36 seconds was just short of the 10.05 that was needed to qualify for the US Men's Olympic team. DK is already looking toward the 2024 Olympics in Paris and possibly qualifying for the US team.

Like many professional athletes, DK Metcalf has also sought to give back through charitable work and events. Interestingly enough, one of DK's first forays into charity as a professional football player actually happened by accident. During a game in his rookie season, ESPN announcer Joe Tessitore accidentally mispronounced DK's name, calling him "Decaf Metcalf."

A Georgia company, Volcanica Coffee, started selling 16-ounce bags of "decaf Metcalf" on its website. Both Tessitore and DK agreed to the deal as long as the proceeds went to charity. Tessitore's half went to the Cystic Fibrosis Foundation. DK's half went to the Prison Fellowship. The Prison Fellowship helps prisoners, former prisoners, and their families in seeking legal counsel and returning to society once they are released. DK also wore cleats with the foundation's logo for the NFL's "My Cleats, My Cause" weekend. The cleats were auctioned off with the proceeds going to the Prison Fellowship.

DK has also donated $25,000 to the Swedish Hospital in Seattle and $25,0000 to a food bank in Oxford, Mississippi. He decided to give back to the two places that helped make him the person and the player that he had become.

Metcalf also had a bit of an embarrassing moment during a charity event. He was playing in a charity softball event in Seattle. Just before the game, he was asked what Major League Baseball player he would compare his game to, and DK responded, "Hank Aaron."

He probably should have chosen someone with a few less home runs. Perhaps someone with none. As it turned out, DK became the only player to strike out in the celebrity softball game. To make matters worse, singer JoJo Siwa, who is more than six inches shorter than DK, hit a double on the next pitch.

So, it looks like DK won't be playing in the MLB anytime soon! Right now, he has his sights set on continuing to dominate the NFL. Not bad for a kid who was told less than five years ago that he would never play football again.

Chapter 5: Legacy

It is hard to pin down a legacy for a player who just turned 25. After only four seasons in the NFL, it would be unexpected and unrealistic for DK Metcalf to be at or near the top of any of the NFL's career leader lists. Currently, he is not in the NFL's top 250 on the career list for receptions, receiving yards, receiving touchdowns, or yards per reception. But there is time.

The Seahawks have also made a change at quarterback that could alter Metcalf's future numbers. Seattle went from the pass-happy offense of Russell Wilson to the run-first, play-action offense of Geno Smith. And to help take some of the pressure off Metcalf, the Seahawks drafted Jaxon Smith-Njigba out of Ohio State this past year. That should help to open up the offense.

In his first three seasons in the league, Metcalf had 3,170 yards and 29 touchdowns. He became one of just eight receivers in NFL history with at least 3,000 yards and 29 touchdowns in their first three seasons. The list of receivers who also accomplished the feat includes Hall-of-Famers Jerry Rice, Randy Moss, and Bob Hayes. This is rarified company, and could be a hint that we will see DK in the Hall of Fame himself one day.

Metcalf's yardage in his first three seasons is also the highest in the history of the Seattle Seahawks. Metcalf is currently eighth on Seattle's all-time receiving yardage list, seventh in receiving touchdowns, and eighth in receptions. He has a long way to go before he catches Hall-of-Famer Steve Largent, but he is off to a good start.

One record that Metcalf could easily break is for the most catches of more than 50 yards in a playoff game. He is currently ranked second with three, tied with Randy Moss. He only needs one more to break the record. What makes Metcalf's accomplishment so remarkable is that he has three catches of more than 50 yards in only four career playoff games.

What is certain is that DK Metcalf will be remembered for his feats of physical strength dating all the way back to his high school career. Metcalf grew up in the age of the internet, and all his accomplishments in the weight room are online for everyone to see.

DK has people wondering how a receiver who is so big can be so fast—a trait that makes him mesmerizing to watch when he takes off down the field. He also has people wondering how it's possible for someone to have less than two percent body fat, as Metcalf claims. His incredible physique coupled with his jaw-dropping speed may also become an integral part of his legacy one day. He proves that you can still be blindingly fast even when you are also very big. Of course, it helps when your size is predicated on a mountain of muscle!

But Metcalf has proven that he is more than just a big body. He is an innately talented wide receiver who is frankly just starting to learn his position. After only 21 games in college due to injury, Metcalf had to relearn everything about the position and do it on the professional level. His ability to overcome a serious neck injury that could have ended his career before it began is also a testament to his dedication and determination to become one of the best. He is really just getting started, but he has already successfully turned himself into an NFL receiver and a borderline great one at that.

Only time will tell just how good DK Metcalf can be. Perhaps someday, he will once again carry the George Halas Trophy off the field, like he did when his father played for the Bears. But this time, he will have earned it himself.

Final Word/About the Author

I was born and raised in Norwalk, Connecticut. Growing up, I could often be found spending many nights watching basketball, soccer, and football matches with my father in the family living room. I love sports and everything that sports can embody. I believe that sports are one of the most genuine forms of competition, heart, and determination. I write my works to learn more about influential athletes in the hopes that from my writing, you the reader can walk away inspired to put in an equal if not greater amount of hard work and perseverance to pursue your goals. If you enjoyed *DK Metcalf: The Inspiring Story of One of Football's Star Wide Receivers,* please leave a review! Also, you can read more of my works on *David Ortiz, Cody Bellinger, Alex Bregman, Francisco Lindor, Shohei Ohtani, Ronald Acuna Jr., Javier Baez, Jose Altuve, Christian Yelich, Max Scherzer, Mookie Betts, Pete Alonso, Clayton Kershaw, Mike Trout, Bryce Harper, Jackie Robinson, Justin Verlander,*

Derek Jeter, Ichiro Suzuki, Ken Griffey Jr., Babe Ruth, Aaron Judge, Novak Djokovic, Roger Federer, Rafael Nadal, Serena Williams, Naomi Osaka, Coco Gauff, Baker Mayfield, George Kittle, Matt Ryan, Matthew Stafford, Eli Manning, Khalil Mack, Davante Adams, Terry Bradshaw, Jimmy Garoppolo, Philip Rivers, Von Miller, Aaron Donald, Joey Bosa, Josh Allen, Mike Evans, Joe Burrow, Carson Wentz Adam Thielen, Stefon Diggs, Lamar Jackson, Dak Prescott, Patrick Mahomes, Odell Beckham Jr., J.J. Watt, Colin Kaepernick, Aaron Rodgers, Tom Brady, Russell Wilson, Peyton Manning, Drew Brees, Calvin Johnson, Brett Favre, Rob Gronkowski, Andrew Luck, Richard Sherman, Bill Belichick, Candace Parker, Skylar Diggins-Smith, A'ja Wilson, Lisa Leslie, Sue Bird, Diana Taurasi, Julius Erving, Clyde Drexler, John Havlicek, Oscar Robertson, Ja Morant, Gary Payton, Khris Middleton, Michael Porter Jr., Julius Randle, Jrue Holiday, Domantas Sabonis, Mike Conley Jr., Jerry West, Dikembe Mutombo, Fred

VanVleet, Jamal Murray, Zion Williamson, Brandon Ingram, Jaylen Brown, Charles Barkley, Trae Young, Andre Drummond, JJ Redick, DeMarcus Cousins, Wilt Chamberlain, Bradley Beal, Rudy Gobert, Aaron Gordon, Kristaps Porzingis, Nikola Vucevic, Andre Iguodala, Devin Booker, John Stockton, Jeremy Lin, Chris Paul, Pascal Siakam, Jayson Tatum, Gordon Hayward, Nikola Jokic, Bill Russell, Victor Oladipo, Luka Doncic, Ben Simmons, Shaquille O'Neal, Joel Embiid, Donovan Mitchell, Damian Lillard, Giannis Antetokounmpo, Chris Bosh, Kemba Walker, Isaiah Thomas, DeMar DeRozan, Amar'e Stoudemire, Al Horford, Yao Ming, Marc Gasol, Draymond Green, Kawhi Leonard, Dwyane Wade, Ray Allen, Pau Gasol, Dirk Nowitzki, Jimmy Butler, Paul Pierce, Manu Ginobili, Pete Maravich, Larry Bird, Kyle Lowry, Jason Kidd, David Robinson, LaMarcus Aldridge, Derrick Rose, Paul George, Kevin Garnett, Michael Jordan, LeBron James, Kyrie Irving, Klay Thompson, Stephen Curry, Kevin Durant, Russell Westbrook,

Chris Paul, Blake Griffin, Kobe Bryant, Anthony Davis, Joakim Noah, Scottie Pippen, Carmelo Anthony, Kevin Love, Grant Hill, Tracy McGrady, Vince Carter, Patrick Ewing, Karl Malone, Tony Parker, Allen Iverson, Hakeem Olajuwon, Reggie Miller, Michael Carter-Williams, James Harden, John Wall, Tim Duncan, Steve Nash, Gregg Popovich, Pat Riley, John Wooden, Steve Kerr, Brad Stevens, Red Auerbach, Doc Rivers, Erik Spoelstra, Mike D'Antoni, and *Phil Jackson* in the Kindle Store. If you love football, check out my website at claytongeoffreys.com to join my exclusive list where I let you know about my latest books and give you lots of goodies.

Like what you read? Please leave a review!

I write because I love sharing the stories of influential athletes like DK Metcalf with fantastic readers like you. My readers inspire me to write more so please do not hesitate to let me know what you thought by leaving a review! If you love books on life, sports, or productivity, check out my website at claytongeoffreys.com to join my exclusive list where I let you know about my latest books. Aside from being the first to hear about my latest releases, you can also download a free copy of *33 Life Lessons: Success Principles, Career Advice & Habits of Successful People*. See you there!

Clayton

References

[i] Fleming, David. "DK Metcalf is Chasing Glory." ESPN the Magazine. Nov. 19, 2020.

[ii] McManus, Tim. "How DK Metcalf Became an Internet-Breaking NFL Wide Receiver Prospect." ESPN.Com. April 2, 2019. Web.

[iii] Cronin, Courtney. "Oxford's Metcalf Learns from a Pro." Clarion Ledge. August 22, 2015.

[iv] Wisniewski, Lindsey. "The Moment DK Metcalf's Father Knew He Created a Monster." NBC Sports.Com Nov. 13, 2020. Web.

[v] Potter, Davis. "Ole Miss Freshman Receiver DK Metcalf Out with a Broken Foot." The Oxford Eagle. Sept. 10, 2016.

[vi] "Ta'amu late TD Rallies Mississippi Past Kentucky 37-34." ESPN.Com. Nov. 4, 2017. Web.

[vii] Suss, Nick. "Ole Miss Wide Receiver DK Metcalf Announces Declaration for NFL Draft." The Clarion Ledger. Nov. 23, 2018.

[viii] "Wilson Throws 5 TDs, Seahawks Outlast Bucs, 40-34, in OT." ESPN.Com. Nov. 3, 2019. Web.

[ix] "Why Did the Eagles Take JJ Arcega-Whiteside Over DK Metcalf?" NBC Sports.Com. Nov. 20, 2019. Web.

[x] "Wilson Leads Seahawks Past Eagles 17-9." ESPN.Com. Jan. 5, 2020. Web.

[xi] Prasad, Aryanna. "Once His Father's Teammate, DK Metcalf Building Bond with Greg Olsen in Seattle." Sports Illustrated. Aug. 10, 2020.

[xii] "Wilson Throws Five More TDs, Seahawks Topple Dallas 38-31." ESPN.Com. Sept. 27, 2020. Web.

[xiii] "Metcalf, Wilson Lead Seahawks Over Eagles, 23-17." ESPN.Com. Nov. 30, 2020. Web.

[xiv] "Rams Get Better of Division Rival, Toping Seahawks 30-20." ESPN.Com. Jan. 5, 2021. Web.

[xv] Schad, Tom. "NFL Receiver DK Metcalf Holds His Own on the Track in 100-M Debut." USA Today. May 9, 2021.

[xvi] Florio, Mike. "Pete Carroll On the Team's Offensive Struggles." NBC Sports.Com. Nov. 17, 2021. Web.

[xvii] "Penny, Metcalf Lead Seahawks in Blowout of Lions, 51-29." ESPN.Com. Jan. 2, 2022. Web.

[xviii] Smith, Corbin. "Seahawks WR Metcalf Shares Photo of Left Foot in Walking Boot." Sports Illustrated. Feb. 14, 2022.

[xix] "Seahawks Trade Russell Wilson to Denver." Seattle Seahawks.Com. March 16, 2022. Web.

[xx] Daniels, Tim. "Seahawks DK Metcalf on Russell Wilson Trade." Bleacher Report. March 25, 2022.

[xxi] Boyle, John. "Seahawks Sign WR DK Metcalf to a Multi-Year Extension." Seattle Seahawks.Com. July 30, 2022. Web.

[xxii] Nasser, Reese. "DK Metcalf Breaks Down Geno Smith's Evolution to QB1 in 2022." Clutch Points.Com. April 14, 2023. Web.

[xxiii] "Seahawks Survive Wilson's Return, Edge Broncos on Missed Field Goal." ESPN.Com. Sept. 13, 2022. Web.

[xxiv] Obee, Maliik. "DK Metcalf Makes History in NFC Wild Card Defeat." Seattle Seahawks.Com. Jan. 15, 2023. Web.

[xxv] Dimmitt, Zach. "Seahawks QB Geno Smith 'Has Kept his Mouth Shut' as Big Contract Awaits." Sports Illustrated. Feb. 19, 2023.

[xxvi] "DK Metcalf Call Out Tyreek Hill, Says He's Been Trying to Race Him for Two Years." Fox Sports.Com. May 25, 2023. Web.

Made in United States
Troutdale, OR
12/31/2023

16586492R00066